THE FIRM YOU WANT

Get Off the Hamster Wheel and Build

An Accountancy or A Bookkeeping Firm

That Runs Without You

(Like I Did)

NIKOLAI NAYLOR

To Peter,
I hope you like the
book.

The Firm You Want

Copyright © Nikolai Naylor

First edition September 2023

ISBN: 979-8-8567- 0856-0

Forward

Hello,

I am excited to introduce you to *The Firm You Want*, the first book by Nikolai Naylor – a successful UK accountant, entrepreneur, and valued member of the Accountants' Mastermind community.

Nikolai's book is a treasure trove of insights and practical advice to help you take your accounting or bookkeeping firm to new heights. Drawing on his own experiences as the owner of **Naylor Accountancy Services and Intelligent Outsourcing**, Nikolai shares the lessons he has learned, the mistakes he has made, and the strategies he has used to create a business that operates efficiently and effectively, even when he is not directly involved in day-to-day operations.

What sets this book apart is its practicality. Nikolai offers actionable steps that you can use to build a firm that works for you. He shows you how to delegate effectively, build a strong team, streamline your processes, and create a sustainable, scalable, and rewarding firm.

As the owner of GreenStones Accountants and The Accountancy Mastermind, I can confidently say that this book is a must-read for anyone who wants to build a successful accounting or bookkeeping firm. Nikolai's expertise extends beyond accounting, and his insights will help you take control of your business and your life.

One of the most inspiring aspects of Nikolai's story is his **growth mindset**. He is always learning, striving to improve, and looking for ways to create more value for his clients and team. This book is a testament to that mindset, and it is **packed with practical advice** that will **help you achieve your goals** and build the firm of your dreams.

The Firm You Want is not just a book to read and set aside. **It is a call to action**. Nikolai's practical advice is designed to help you create a firm that works for you, and the ONLY way to achieve that is to **TAKE ACTION** on what you learn from these pages.

Nikolai Naylor and Simon Chaplin

So, I challenge you to put Nikolai's advice into practice. Use this book as a **roadmap to build the business of your dreams**, and don't be afraid to take risks, experiment, and iterate along the way. Building a successful accounting or bookkeeping firm takes hard work, dedication, and a willingness to try new things. But with Nikolai's guidance, you can do it.

As someone who has owned an accountancy practice for over two decades and worked with many practice owners, I can tell you that the rewards of building a successful business are immense. Not just financial rewards but the satisfaction of creating something that provides real value to your clients and your team.

So, **read this book, TAKE ACTION, and build *The Firm You Want*.** I wish you all the best on your journey, and I know you can achieve great things with Nikolai's guidance.

Let's Get Started...

Simon Chaplin

Owner at GreenStones Accountants and Founder of The Accountants' Mastermind.

Contents

About the Author

Nikolai Naylor has run his own UK accountancy firm, Naylor Accountancy Services, since 2012 after giving up working in the City of London.

Nikolai always knew he wanted to have his own business at some point. He did not know what or when though. He wanted to make a difference and did not feel he could do this in a big corporation. After being inspired by a friend whose accountancy practice made a significant difference to businesses, he set up his own firm. Like every other entrepreneur, Nikolai had to start by doing everything himself. However he gradually built a team as he could afford it. Crucially, he started creating a structure which allowed his business to operate without him.

As with anything in life, the journey has not been smooth, and there will be more bumps in the road. He sees these bumps as learnings along the way.

Nikolai has another business, Intelligent Outsourcing, which he started in 2016. Based in the Philippines, it supplies accountancy and bookkeeping firms with offshore teams that work exclusively for them. This partnership allows these firms to focus on client relationships and added value work, enabling them to grow. He has a great team running the business in the Philippines and is frequently there. With Nikolai's desire to make a difference not only to his partners/clients and the team, Intelligent Outsourcing also does outreach work in the local community with a focus on helping educate people out of poverty.

Nikolai is married with two teenage children and a dog. He loves spending time with them, especially on holidays where distractions don't exist. He travelled the world for over a year with his wife shortly after getting married, which was a great way to start married life. They did a month's volunteering in Ecuador, then travelled around Latin America for six months learning Spanish, followed by Fiji, the Cook Islands, New Zealand, Australia, Vietnam, Cambodia, Thailand and Malaysia.

Nikolai is a 4th degree black belt in Tae Kwon Do, having practised it since he was a teenager, and he goes to classes regularly with his son and daughter. Well-being is essential to him and he adheres to a daily routine.

Nikolai enjoys learning. He completed his degree in Business Studies at Leeds Beckett University. He then studied accounting with the Chartered Institute of Management Accountants and treasury with the Association of Corporate Treasurers while working. Nikolai now focuses on self-development and consumes loads of different material on diverse topics. He also finds being part of a mastermind group helps with self-development.

He loved travelling and backpacking around Europe and the USA whilst a student. After university he travelled around the world, starting in India, Nepal, and South-East Asia. He stopped in Australia to work in Sydney for six months before resuming his travels around Australia and New Zealand, finishing with Fiji, Hawaii, LA, and New York.

If you are wondering where the name 'Nikolai' comes from, it is Danish, as his mother is from Denmark. He visits Denmark at least once a year to see his family. Nikolai speaks Danish with an English accent, as he mainly grew up in Yorkshire.

Introduction

I have read loads of books and experimented with different ways of operating my accountancy firm, Naylor Accountancy Services. We are currently operating in a way which enables me to step back and focus on strategy and guidance. The team does the day-to-day work, allowing me to focus on my other business, Intelligent Outsourcing.

Nothing in this book is rocket science. It will not rock the world with fantastic new ideas. It simply contains the knowledge I have gained so far in my journey which has allowed me to create the accountancy firm I have now and given me the freedom to focus on what I prefer to spend my time on.

It is not perfect. We are continually improving how we do things and I am constantly learning.

This book is a shortcut. I hope it inspires you to create the accounting or bookkeeping firm you want. This book goes through what we have done in my accountancy practice to get **the firm I want,** which is independent of me. You can use this book like a menu and pick and choose where you prefer to start and gradually add on as you progress. The most important thing for me is to share **how you can get your accountancy or bookkeeping firm 'working for you' rather than 'you working' for your firm**.

30 Ways to Ensure You Fail!

Before we go through the positive things that you can do to improve your accountancy or bookkeeping firm, it is **important to know the ways you can fail to run your firm effectively**. None of us are perfect, and you will no doubt see things here that you may be doing now or may have done in the past.

How can you ensure you have a bad business, are stressed, do all the work, never take a holiday, earn little and ensure you are bored as you are only doing compliance work?

This may seem back to front to you, but knowing how you will fail to have the business you desire is key to understanding what you must do to get the accountancy or bookkeeping firm you deserve if you put in the work and effort.

What 30 things do you need to do to fail?

1. **Never delegate** as you think no one can work as well as you or manage relationships better than you, so never allow anyone else to do anything. Take on everything yourself.

2. **Do work for free**. Do it as a favour or because it takes little time to do and you know exactly what to do as you have studied accounting for years and have the necessary expertise. Why should the client pay when it is so easy for you to do it?

3. **Forget to invoice for work that you agreed a fee on**. You are so busy doing everything that you need more time to invoice clients for your work. So, you get stressed and work loads of hours for free. You do

not like to invoice as it feels dirty; you like the client and value the friendship, so do not feel you should invoice despite having agreed a fee.

4. **Do not chase outstanding payments**. You are so busy you have no time to chase anyone, so you just ignore the build of debtors and carry on doing work for those owing you money. Again, you are okay with doing work for free as you are sure the client will realise they need to pay you soon.

5. **Carry on doing work for clients who don't pay and do not intend to pay you**. So, continue to work for free, be stressed and take time away from paying clients to work with non-paying clients.

6. **Put free work or non-paying clients ahead of those paying on time.** So, you will have less time for paying clients and less time to bring in new paying clients as you spend your valuable time on non-paying work and clients.

7. **Never increase fees**. You have no time for fee reviews, so you are happy to carry on charging the startup fee when your client's business was earning less than £50K even though it is now earning £250K per annum and bookkeeping has increased tenfold.

8. **Allow scope creep.** It is painful for you to do a fee review with clients. You feel uncomfortable, the client may not take it well and they may leave if you increase fees.

9. **Never push yourself out of your comfort zone.** This means you will never move anything forward unless you already feel comfortable with it and know it.

10. **You are worried about clients leaving.** So, you do whatever clients say even if they are wrong, or you end up doing extra work for free.

11. **Keep clients who are unpleasant or cost you money.** These may be clients who are unwilling to pay for the service they are consuming, are always late with information, and blame you and your team for delays. In other words, no mutual respect.

12. **Do not get rid of poor-performing team members**. Allow bad apples in your team to continue bringing everyone else down and have no respect for you or the business or clients. Permit them to create negativity in the team.

13. **You have everything in your head** about clients, processes, procedures and your plans. You know how everything needs to be done, so you do not see the need to set these out in writing once you have trained your team members. They only have the process in their heads as well.

14. **Everyone uses their own processes with nothing written down**. You do not worry if any of your team is off as they will just catch up when they get back, and if the team member should never come back, you are sure another team member will be able to work out what they are doing and create their own new process in their head.

15. **Never learn from mistakes or admit them.** You will not admit to your mistakes as you are the boss, and your ego will not allow you to be seen as making mistakes.

16. **Your team never learns from their mistakes**. You do not worry about it and you do not put new processes and procedures or training in place to ensure it does not happen again.

17. **You do not trust anyone**. You must micro-manage everything because you cannot trust your team to do the work.

18. **You have no plan for your business.** You have no idea what you want to do in the next 12 months, let alone the next five to ten years.

19. **Procrastinate** about everything so you only decide once it is too late.

20. **Only work to the HMRC and Companies House deadline.** You do not care about getting work done and submitted as quickly as possible as you think clients are fine being told their payments are to be made to HMRC the day before it is required with no prior warning.

21. **Never listen to clients, ignoring their needs and concerns.** You only tell your clients what you think they want to hear. You are only concerned about getting the work done, telling them what to pay HMRC, and then moving on to the next job.

22. **Never listen to your team.** You never have 1:1 meetings with your team as you see it as a waste of time.

23. **Do not keep up with changes in accounting regulations** and tax laws.

24. **Do not train your team.** You do not provide your team with ongoing professional development opportunities.

25. **Communicate ineffectively.** Both with your team and clients.

26. **Do not invest in technology** to streamline your firm's operations.

27. **Have no idea of your finances** or keep track of your expenses.

28. **Have no vision** for your business.

29. **Do not track your performance**, set goals, or have KPIs.

30. **Do not invest in your own personal and professional development.**

I am sure you will see some of the above in your life now or in the past. If you don't, then are you being honest with yourself? I know I have exhibited most of the above at some point. I now positively work to avoid them.

Chapter 1

YOU

1. YOU

What Do You Want from Your Firm?

Do you want an accountancy or bookkeeping firm which doesn't rely entirely on you?

Do you want a firm that allows you to sleep at night without worrying that Jones and Sons had their accounts filed on time?

Do you want a team that can do everything needed in your business without you even being there?

In short, do you want a business that will look after your clients and continue making money while you re-charge your batteries and spend quality time with your family?

I know many accountants who have their own practice who work all the hours possible to keep their clients happy and put their friends and family second. I was one of them. When you first start your accountancy or bookkeeping firm, this is normal as you must do everything until you have a sufficient client base to warrant getting more team members to help you. However, most accountants never more on from this.

For business owners, the **main goal is to have a business which is a 'turn-key business' that can operate without you being there**. This means that you can focus on what you want to do and easily sell your business.

Is this what you want from your firm?

There are **three freedoms** that we may want in any combination which are:

1. **Financial** freedom – wanting a certain amount of income to enjoy a particular lifestyle. It is vital to know what lifestyle you want. I have met many people who set themselves financial targets which are well in excess of what they need to enjoy their chosen lifestyle. This means they are going to take on far more risk and spend a lot more time working than if they had aimed just above what they actually needed. There is nothing wrong with paying yourself £1-million+ a year. I know several people who do. However, it requires sacrifice and risk-taking. Focus on what you want to earn for your preferred lifestyle and then look to see if you want to exchange your time and take on more risk to earn more.

2. **Time** freedom – wanting more time to focus on things that are important to you and not just spending time on your business. This could be family, a hobby, travel, study, strategy, … whatever it is for you.

3. **Mind** freedom – wanting peace of mind that all clients are being well looked after and all filings are done on time. All without you needing to get involved.

You may enjoy the technical accounting work, so you can always focus on that and get others to focus on the client-facing responsibilities. If you love dealing with client relationships, focus on that and get others in the team to do the work for the clients.

Wake Up and Smell the Coffee!

Before even looking at creating **the Firm You Want**, you have to realise that you are the reason you do not have the firm you want... clear and simple. **Do not blame anyone or anything else.** Take full responsibility for the fact you work too many hours, do not see your family, are always thinking of your clients and are worried about losing clients and income. If you do not do this, you will never get the firm you want.

> "Take chances, make mistakes. That's how you grow."
>
> *Mary Tyler Moore*

I realised that **I was the bottleneck** to growing my accountancy firm, Naylor Accountancy Services. I had to change my mindset and the structure of the business to step away and get the firm I wanted. This has not been easy to do, and I wanted to write this book to give other accountants tips on what I have learnt so far. I say so far because I know we have loads more to do to improve things, and I will be learning throughout the journey as we grow Naylor Accountancy Services. This will be through continuous self-development, the leadership team enlightening me and us learning from mistakes that we all inevitably make. **You should never be complacent and think you have it all worked out**. Things are constantly changing. The key is to stay relevant and continuously improve.

This quote is so apt and I am sure you can relate to this.

> *"The only real mistake is the one from which we learn nothing,"*
>
> Henry Ford

I also like these words of wisdom given by a Hall of Fame basketball player/coach:

> "If you're not making mistakes, then you're not doing anything."
>
> *John Wooden*

Later in the book, you will see that it is vital to allow mistakes to be made by your team and ensure they learn from them to develop and take jobs from you. I know accountants who, as soon as someone makes a mistake they say, "I knew I should have done it myself. The team member just doesn't know how to do it," or "They will never learn." This approach will guarantee that you never get the firm you want.

See sections **'Let Go!'** and **'Team' for practical advice on how to avoid this common fate.**

The realisation of what you want and what you need to do is critical. Some people are happy the way their business is as it gives them the income and lifestyle they want which is great! However, as you are reading this book, I am certain that you have yet to build the company of your dreams.

Please allow me to be blunt. If you do not change anything or you are blaming circumstances that you feel are out of your control, then **you will never get the firm you want.** You have to **"wake up and smell the coffee"** and realise **you are in control**. You are accountable for your own success. Only you can make the required changes. There are many business owners who read books, attend seminars and listen to podcasts and yet fail to get results. This is not because the advice was poor. It was simply because they did not act on it. **Knowledge is not power. It is potential.** It only delivers results when applied.

Most people do not like change. Sometimes, you must experience pain that is intense enough for you to make a change. Unless, of course, you are very forward-looking and have a vision for you and your business that pushes you to make the changes with a plan. If you read and implement the recommendations in this book, you will join a select group of forward-thinking accountants. Membership is not exclusive. It is there for anyone who is prepared to find out more about what makes a firm successful and then implement what they have learned.

You Cannot Make Everyone Happy!

The simple truth is that you cannot make everyone happy. You must do what is right and consider others, but that does not mean you have to do what others want you to do.

You must never be afraid of making people unhappy as some people do not like change and everyone has their own opinion. You should listen to what other people have to say and consider their input, but you must make up your own mind on what you want to do and then go for it.

Business owners and entrepreneurs by definition are rule breakers. They do not go with the crowd. The crowd being the vast majority of working age people who are either employed by the public or private sector or who do not have a job.

Some team members and clients will not be happy with change but speak with them and potentially lose them to move forward.

Story of a team member against change

I had a Naylor Accountancy Services team member, John, who was totally against having an offshoring team. He was always negative, saying "The Filipino team will not know where to allocate a Boots receipt when they do the bookkeeping." My answer was always straightforward, "They will use Google and learn."

John also hated our daily huddles when we started them. He had a face like thunder throughout all the meetings making his displeasure clear to all including our offshore team in the Philippines.

I point-blank refuse to compromise our development for any team member so we parted ways. If I had compromised, we would not have the business we have today or our successful offshoring company, Intelligent Outsourcing.

Let Go!

Letting go is the most difficult for accountants, especially as we like to be in control and think we are the best at it. We do not want to trust someone else to do the project or to ensure things are done on time. We want to do it.

We think we are the only person who can deal with a specific client. In some cases, this may be true, but first let go and then if you still want to keep a client that is kicking off, go back to meeting with them but get all the work done by the team. Your team will only learn to do the work you are doing once **you allow them to do it and train them in it**, so proactively ensure you delegate and train the team members in what you do and let go so they become responsible for carrying out the job.

I used to do all the limited company annual filings, setups and changes at Companies House for address, directors, shares, etc. I carried on doing this even though I had hired Dee full-time to do bookkeeping and some other administrative work. Then a year in, when I was swamped with work, I gave Dee a small Company Secretariat job. She did it well and asked me why I had not given her that type of work sooner. I realised then that I thought I was the only one who could do the work as no one else could figure it out... **how wrong was I**? Why did I even think like that? So, I gave Dee all the Company Secretariat tasks. She did it for years before we handed it over to our administrative team, Karen and Leslie, in our Intelligent Outsourcing offshore team for Naylor Accountancy Services. They do a great job and can figure out anything using our Company Secretariat system. I **let go** and put **trust** in the people to whom I **delegated** the work to. They became **accountable** for the work willingly, giving them empowerment.

Vision

As a business owner, **you must know what you want from your accountancy or bookkeeping firm.** Look at what you enjoy doing, what income you need to take out of the business, how much time you want to spend with family and friends, and what holidays you would like to go on.

As a business owner, you must be clear about what you want before you can guide others towards a vision of the future that the team will be part of. Once you have a Leadership Team in place, you must create the Vision Statement with them in your **Annual Way Forward** meeting. This is key to getting the leadership team's buy-in and allows them to highlight issues and barriers you may not have considered.

What do you want the business to look like in 10 years? This is the first thing to focus on, as once you have this, then you know what it should look like in three years which makes the 12-month plan much easier to create. It is incredible what you can achieve if you look out 10 years... You can think big if you and your leadership team want that. You may be more interested in maintaining what you have with you while working fewer hours and having your 'A-team' run your business for you. However, if you open up the creation and maintenance of the vision to your Leadership Team, you will be surprised by what they come up with. They will also be far more engaged with the business and its development. After all, it will increase their earning capacity within the business and give them self-development with the accompanying feeling of achievement and self-worth.

I have been told that others have a 5-year vision and then go back from there. However, to me, this is too limiting as you can clearly achieve much more in 10 years as opposed to five.

If you only focus on five years, you will not know your ultimate destination. With 10 years, you really can play around and work out what you, your Leadership Team and your business should look like. Ten years is good because you can then plan back what you need to do to get there. By thinking about your journey, opportunities and ideas will pop up which may never have appeared if you were limited to five years.

Having said all this, if you want to focus on 5-year goals, then do that. You may be coming up to retirement and may not be interested in growth. I love looking to the future and have always planned to build a legacy business that will outlast me, so I want to look as far ahead as possible.

This is a fundamental way to create your Vision. You want it to become something you can see, feel and experience as if you are already there. So, the more detail, the better. After all, it is your Vision. A picture of what you want you, your Leadership Team and your business to look like in the future.

> "A vision is a compass that guides you through the journey of building a successful business."
>
> *Simon Sinek*

Your Leadership

Leadership is all about influence and requires followers. You must get your team on-board with your Vision and ensure they have the motivation to move towards it through executing the plan.

You cannot create anything of value with just one person. You need a team for that. That is why leadership is all about influence.

John Maxwell, probably the world's biggest expert on leadership, says:

> *"Everything rises and falls on leadership."*
>
> *John Maxwell*

As a leader, always look at how you can add value to your team members. This could be giving them advice, connecting them with others, giving them a project to develop them, giving them more responsibility and letting them know when they have made a mistake and asking them what they learned from it and what would they do differently next time.

Look to create leaders within your business as this will allow you to ensure someone is taking responsibility for certain areas and you will be able to take items off your long list. To be a truly great leader you must create and develop leaders, not just have minions. If you are always the hero, then the business will only be able to sustain itself if you are there as you are the only one who knows it all. This can crush others as you will probably not allow them to air their views and instead just tell them what to do and how to do to it.

You must be a **multiplier** not a **diminisher** as a leader.

The terms 'leadership multiplier' and 'leadership diminisher' were coined by Liz Wiseman in her book *Multipliers: How the Best Leaders Make Everyone Smarter*. These terms refer to two distinct types of leaders and their impact on their teams.

A **leadership multiplier** is a leader who amplifies the intelligence and capabilities of their team. Multipliers create a culture of trust and empowerment, encourage team members to take ownership of their work, and provide opportunities for learning and growth. Multipliers seek to bring out the best in their team members and help them reach their full potential.

In contrast, a **leadership diminisher** is a leader who restricts the intelligence and capabilities of their team. Diminishers tend to micromanage, hoard information, and create a culture of fear and dependency. Diminishers often think they know best and don't trust their team members to make decisions. As a result, team members may feel disempowered, undervalued, and unmotivated.

Story of a diminisher

I acquired an accountancy practice and Mary, the previous owner, was a diminisher. Mary did not believe anyone could do the accounts and file them correctly or do the invoicing. Mary had to do it all.

The practice was in a real mess when we took it over and all the accounts were being done up to 12 months after the year end. They had changed the year end dates by a day at Companies House which allowed an extra three months on top of the normal 9-month filing deadline.

Mary had not invoiced many clients for work they had completed in previous years so she was stressed doing work for clients for zero money!!! Had Mary allowed other accountants that worked for the company to invoice once they had completed the work, do peer reviews and allowed the team to do some of the accounts and submit them to HMRC and Companies House, then she would probably not have had to sell the business.

Mary was selling as she could not cope with running the practice. She did not empower her team and she constantly blamed others for anything that went wrong.

The evidence suggests that **leadership multipliers are generally more effective** than leadership diminishers. This is because multipliers create an environment in which everyone can contribute to their full potential, which leads to better results, increased engagement, and higher levels of creativity and innovation. By contrast, leadership diminishers may limit the potential of their teams, leading to lower morale, less productivity, and missed opportunities.

Here are some examples of leaders who are considered to be leadership multipliers:

Satya Nadella, CEO of Microsoft – Satya is known for his ability to empower his team members and encourage them to take risks and innovate. He has created a culture of collaboration and openness which has led to Microsoft's recent successes.

Mary Barra, CEO of General Motors – Mary is known for her focus on empowering her team members and creating a culture of trust and transparency. She has worked to break down silos within the organisation and encourage cross-functional collaboration.

Reed Hastings, CEO of Netflix – Reed is known for his ability to attract and retain top talent, as well as his focus on innovation and experimentation. He encourages his team members to take ownership of their work and provides opportunities for learning and growth.

In contrast, here are some examples of leaders who are considered to be leadership diminishers:

1. The late **Steve Jobs**, Co-founder of Apple – Steve was known for his micromanagement and his tendency to hoard information. He was a brilliant innovator, but his leadership style could be limiting to his team members. Watch the *Steve Jobs movie* for more information.

2. **Jeff Immelt**, former CEO of General Electric – Jeff was criticised for his tendency to centralise decision-making and his focus on short-term

results. He was seen as a leader who limited the potential of his team members.

3. **Travis Kalanick**, former CEO of Uber – Travis was known for his aggressive leadership style and his tendency to create a culture of fear and aggression. He was criticised for his treatment of team members and for limiting the potential of his team members.

As the leader of your accountancy or bookkeeping firm, you must think about who you want to develop internally as a leader and if you need to bring in someone from outside to take on a leadership role. You may want someone you can develop and mold or you may prefer someone who can come straight in and get on delivering with little guidance. If you are a small firm, you may not be in a position to develop a Leadership Team but you must think of your leadership style and your impact on others.

> "Leadership is the capacity to translate vision into reality."
>
> *Warren Bennis*

Believe

You must **believe in yourself, the vision and others**. This is absolutely critical! If you do not believe in yourself, then you have no hope in getting others to buy into your plans.

This means you must believe that you are capable of achieving what you are setting out to accomplish with a plan and team in place to do it. You must believe you have the skillset needed and if you are missing any knowledge, you must believe you can learn it. Of course, you must then learn whatever you are lacking knowledge in as part of your personal plan.

Once you believe in yourself, your capabilities and your knowledge then you need to ensure you **believe in the Vision** for the business and that it is achievable in the timescales you have set. You must believe 100% in your Vision and focus on it. If you do not believe in the Vision, you will make excuses as to why you are not going to make it rather than create solutions to get you there.

> *"Believe you can and you're halfway there."*
>
> *Theodore Roosevelt*

Finally, you must have a **team that you believe in** and is able to get you to where you want to go. You will more than likely need to bring more team members in and change team members' roles as you grow and progress towards your 10-year vision. The key is to have a team in place that you believe will be able to learn and develop to help you move along your plan for the business. The team members will then feel that you believe in them and they will step up. If team members don't, then you will need to have a conversation with them and that is a different issue (See Letter of Expectation).

Trust Others

This is key to growing **the firm you want** and being able to let go and delegate projects and responsibilities. First, you need to believe the team member can do what is required and then you need to trust them to do whatever it is you need them to do and give them autonomy where required.

They may not execute projects perfectly to start with as team members have to learn and they may not be as efficient as you are. You may lose touch with the coal face (what is happening with every client), but you must trust others as this makes them grow and develop!

Team members will take on the responsibility you give them if they have your business's core values and are capable (See **Build an A-Team**). If team members don't have your core values and are not capable, should you have them in your team at all? Trusting others is similar to believing in others, the difference is you cannot trust someone in your team if you do not believe they are capable of doing the project etc.

You can believe in someone and still not trust them to do something but this is your issue! You must trust in order to 'let go.' Trust can be misplaced. If it is, then re-assess and take the action required.

Story of not trusting your team

I mentioned the practice I acquired earlier on. The previous owner, Mary, did not trust her team to complete projects, file accounts or to invoice for work completed. Mary was convinced that she was the only one capable of doing all of these things. She was a massive bottleneck and to boot she did not operate any systems and procedure (See **Create Systems and Procedures**).

If Mary had **trusted and believed in the team** she would not have been stressed and have had to do everything last minute. This is bad for anyone's wellbeing as well as providing a poor service to the client.

If you trust others, then others are more likely to trust you. We all have accounting or bookkeeping firms and our clients must trust us for them to share with us the data and information they do. So, the quicker someone trusts you the more likely you will take them on as a client.

If you cannot trust your team to do jobs, then how can clients trust you and the team? Trust goes many ways and before people trust you, you must trust them.

"People do business with people they know, like and TRUST."

Dale Carnegie.

Mistakes Are Inevitable So Allow Them

You and your team will make mistakes and you cannot stop that however hard you try. Most entrepreneurs will agree that without making mistakes they would not be where they are today. The reason for this is that businesspeople learn from mistakes and make sure as much as possible that they don't happen again.

So do not beat yourself up or get mad at team members for making them, allow them to make mistakes.

The key to your team members making mistakes is they must learn from them and not make the same mistake again. This is the same for you.

As Henry Ford famously said, **"The only real mistake is the one from which we learn nothing**."

When you and your team make mistakes, everyone must own up to them straight away and not hide them. You want everyone to be open and if they know you are not going to discipline them for making a mistake and view mistakes as inevitable and that you want everybody to learn from them, then team members will be open. I have one caveat with my team. **We will always support them with anything they have done provided they did not violate any of our core values.**

> "The only real mistake is the one from which we learn nothing."
>
> *Henry Ford*

We have what we call 'Project Perfect' which is where we record all mistakes made. This enables us to see what has gone wrong centrally. Then in our weekly meeting, we discuss the issue that created the mistake and once we have got to the bottom of it then we look to see what solution we can implement to ensure that it does not happen again. This could mean adding an extra step to one of our processes, ensuring everyone gets training in a certain element, etc.

> "More people would learn from their mistakes if they weren't so busy denying them."
>
> *Tom Ziglar*

You do not want team members to go below the line and deny a mistake or blame others for it. **You want everyone including yourself to take ownership of mistakes and issues**. This is the only way for you and your team members to improve and take action to ensure the same mistake does not happen again.

> "Smart people learn from their mistakes. But the real sharp ones learn from the mistakes of others."
>
> *Brandon Mull*

Story of not admitting mistakes

Mary, the previous owner of the accountancy firm I acquired, would never admit any mistakes she had made and blamed others. I realised this straight away as it is important in our team to take ownership of what we do and what we are responsible for. We call team members out if they blame, deny or make excuses for anything they are accountable for.

This blaming by Mary covered virtually everything, from why the firm was in such a mess to why clients were leaving. The worst was she was blaming the clients as well as her team.

As a business owner, you are ultimately responsible for the firm, mistakes and issues. As an owner, you must learn from mistakes and develop yourself, your team and your business. Mary thought she was perfect and that only others make mistakes, so it must be their fault.

The problem with not owning up to your own mistakes is that you never improve yourself which impacts your business

I learned a lot of painful lessons from the acquisition. I worked long hours and the team worked constantly to improve everything and we turned it all around in less than a year. I would never want to go through the pain of that acquisition again! But I would not change what happened as I and the rest of the team learned so much. It made us realise how good and robust our systems and procedures are.

I share my stories so that you can learn from my mistakes as well as what I have found to work for me on my journey.

Energy

As the owner of a business, you must have the energy to ensure you can run your business. You also want the energy to spill over to others so they see the urgency in matters that require it.

The key is your well-being. So, ensure you get enough sleep, keep fit and eat healthily. I am not going to go into any details here as I am not a personal trainer or wellbeing guru, but I will give some tips and examples that work for me.

Exercise is any movement of your body, from a regular gentle walk to boxercise, whatever you do is good, just do something.

Stretching is really good for you and worth doing regularly. Stretching and some exercise helps you with those back and neck pains you get from sitting in front of a computer too much. Do not sit for hours as you must move your body. Consider getting a standing desk, answer calls standing up, stand up in meetings, get up to get drinks, walk to talk to people in your office instead of messaging them, this all helps.

The key is not to just sit all day, for example, you drive to work sitting in your car, then sit all day at your desk at work. Then you go home to sit and eat dinner followed by sitting to watch TV. We all do a lot of sitting! Look to fit in at least 30 minutes a day to do some form of exercise which does not involve sitting.

When you need energy bursts do a *'starfish.'* This is lying on the ground with your legs apart and arms apart like a starfish and resting, closing your eyes. Only do this for up to 20 minutes, so like a nap. It is like recharging your batteries. Once you get up, you feel like you have so much more energy. I do this when I get back from work and I am shattered, especially if I will be going to my Tae Kwon Do class that evening.

'Starfish' lying on the floor, (not my best look...)

Before doing an online seminar or online meeting you need to have the energy to jump up and down to get your blood pumping, it gives you more life and you will come across as livelier.

If you need all the attendees of a meeting to forget whatever else they have on their mind and focus on the meeting then get them all to do three deep breaths at the start of a meeting. I have done this on a few occasions in our leadership weekly meetings, be aware your Ds in the DiSC profile will not like this so much (See Chapter in **Team on Profiling**).

Sleeping is so critical to your health, productivity and general well-being. You can still perform relatively well if you have not eaten for 24 hours, but if you have not slept for 24 hours then that has a massive impact on you. Again, I am no expert on this but here are a few tips I have learned:

- **Never turn the light on once you have gone to bed.** So, if you go to the toilet, refrain from turning the light on as it will wake you up from your groggy state and it takes ages to get back to sleep. I learnt this whilst at university as I was really bad at sleeping at night. It has meant that I walk around in the dark and have to feel my way around. If I am in a hotel where I am not used to the layout, this can be interesting when locating the toilet... I've walked into the doors and whacked my shins... So, I never pee standing up at night, as I am sure my accuracy is no good in the dark, so a top tip for men is to sit down while you urinate at night so you don't need to turn the light on. Sorry if that is too much to share, but it is a top tip.
- **Blue light is bad.** Do not look at your devices before bed and certainly turn them off.
- **Have a dark and cool room.** It is best to have the window on a latch to let some fresh air in.
- **Do not drink coffee or have caffeine at least six hours** before you go to bed and a lot of people say do not have it after noon. It all depends on your tolerance to caffeine.

- **Avoid large meals, nicotine, and alcohol before bedtime.** These substances can disrupt your sleep and prevent you from feeling fully rested.
- **Do not eat sugary things before bed,** nuts or other slow-release foods are best if you must eat something.

> *"Energy and persistence conquer all things."*
>
> Benjamin Franklin

Perseverance

Be stubborn and keep going. Keep improving as a person, keep believing in what you are doing and keep working towards your Vision. Life and business are a roller coaster, and you have to take the downs as well as the ups. If you are not happy doing this, then you are more suited to being an employee than a business owner. As an owner, you will have times when you may think "Why am I doing this?" I know I have. It is important you keep focused.

Perseverance is important in any business because it allows you to stay focused on your goals, overcome obstacles, and persist through challenging times. To be successful with your accountancy or bookkeeping firm you must understand that setbacks and failures are inevitable, but with perseverance, you can learn from these experiences and move forward towards achieving your Vision.

Several famous business writers advocate the importance of perseverance in business, including:

- **Stephen Covey** – the author of the best-selling book *The 7 Habits of Highly Effective People*, which emphasises the importance of **persistence** and determination in achieving success.
- **Napoleon Hill** – best known for his book *Think and Grow Rich*, which is based on the idea that success is achieved through **persistence** and the refusal to give up in the face of adversity.
- **Seth Godin** – a prolific writer and speaker on topics related to marketing and entrepreneurship. He often emphasises the importance of **perseverance** and resilience in the face of failure.

> *"Many of life's failures are people who did not realise how close they were to success when they gave up."*
>
> *Thomas Edison*

No Procrastination

Procrastination can be a major obstacle to success in any business, as it can lead to missed opportunities, unmet deadlines, and a general lack of productivity. To achieve success for your business, it is important to avoid procrastination and stay focused on your goals and tasks.

It is important to realise that some personality styles (See **Chapter on Team**) will take longer to come to decisions as they will want to analyse, talk through things, do research, etc. before they will naturally come to a decision. As the business owner, it is your responsibility to push these people forward. This means allowing them some time to deliberate but not so much time as it becomes an issue.

I have this with some members of my Intelligent Outsourcing Leadership Team. It can be frustrating as I can see a clear way forward but I need to bring them with me. I have had to drag some team members along a certain path on occasions. They did not like that, which meant they were not 100% bought into the decision. On one occasion it was costing the business £500 per month, so I could not allow it to continue. If I had allowed the team member to procrastinate further, it would have cost the business more money and no decision would have been made.

It is key to make a decision and act. The decision may not be the right one but if it is not, you either make it the right one or change the decision. This is much better than doing nothing. The important thing is to decide and move forward.

Some of the most famous business writers advocate the importance of avoiding procrastination including some of my favourite authors such as:

- **Brian Tracy** – a motivational speaker and author who has written extensively on the topic of productivity and time management. His book *Eat That Frog!* emphasises the importance of tackling the most difficult tasks first and avoiding procrastination.

- **Stephen Covey** – as mentioned earlier, is the author of *The 7 Habits of Highly Effective People*. One of the habits he emphasises is, "Begin with the end in mind," which encourages individuals to focus on their goals and take action quickly to achieve them.

- **Tony Robbins** – is a well-known motivational speaker and author who often highlights the importance of taking immediate action to achieve success. He argues that procrastination is a major obstacle to success and that acting quickly is essential for achieving one's goals.

> *"You may delay, but time will not."*
>
> *Benjamin Franklin*

Change Course If You Must

Business and life are a journey towards a vision and things change so you may need to change your plans. For example, you suddenly realise your satnav is taking you down a dirt track to nowhere or worse, directing you off a cliff.

Some people will carry on the dirt track until they realise, they are lost. Others will keep going further and further off track as they have a plan and must follow it. Yes, you must create a plan and follow it, but you must be aware if you are on the wrong track and make necessary changes.

It is important to have a plan, but it is equally important to be willing to adjust that plan as circumstances change. Here are some things that could make it necessary to change your business plan:

- **Market conditions**: If the market changes, for example, if a new competitor enters the market, or there is a change in consumer demand, the business plan may need to be adjusted to reflect these new conditions.

- **Financial considerations**: If the business is not meeting its financial targets, the plan may need to be revised to address the issues that are preventing the business from achieving its goals.

- **Internal factors**: Changes in personnel, processes, or technology can all impact the business plan, and may require adjustments to ensure that the plan remains relevant and achievable.

- **External factors**: Political, economic, or social changes can also impact a business plan. For example, changes in regulations or trade policies can impact a business's ability to operate in certain markets and may require adjustments to the plan. This wan seen recently through the Covid lockdowns.

I have had to ensure we change our business plans in Naylor Accountancy Services and Intelligent Outsourcing when I could see there was a major issue. Some in the leadership team were not happy as we set out the plan at the start of the year in our Annual Way Forward meeting. Be aware of people's personality profiles so you are aware of which team members struggle with change. Again, this highlights the need to profile your team, **(See the Chapter on Team)** as this helps to understand how best to interact with them and bring them on-board.

In summary, it is important to have a plan, but it is equally important to be willing to adjust that plan as circumstances change. By staying flexible and adapting to new conditions, you can stay competitive and achieve your goals over the long term.

> *"Failed plans should not be interpreted as a failed vision.*
> *Visions don't change, they are only refined.*
>
> *Plans rarely stay the same and*
>
> *are scrapped or adjusted as needed.*
>
> *Be stubborn about the vision,*
>
> *but flexible with your plan."*
>
> *John C. Maxwell*

Ego

Keeping your ego in check is essential. This allows you to make rational decisions and prioritise the success of your business over personal pride or ego.

> *"Check your ego at the door.*
>
> *The ego can be the great success inhibitor. It can kill opportunities, and it can kill success."*
>
> Dwayne Johnson (The Rock)

If you let your ego get in the way, it can lead to a variety of negative outcomes, including:

- **Poor decision-making**: When you let your ego take over, you may make decisions that are not in the best interest of the business but rather based on personal preferences or desires.
- **Lack of teamwork**: If you have a big ego, it can make it difficult to work with others effectively. You may be more concerned with getting your own way than working collaboratively with your team to achieve the best outcomes.
- **Inability to learn and grow**: Having a big ego can make it difficult to take feedback or criticism, which can hinder your ability to learn and grow as a business owner.

- **Damage to relationships**: If you let your ego get in the way of your interactions with team members, partners, or clients, it can damage relationships and ultimately harm your business.

In contrast, when you keep your ego in check, you are better able to make decisions that prioritise the success of your firm, work effectively with others in your team, learn and grow, and maintain positive relationships. **It allows you to stay humble, open-minded, and receptive to feedback,** all of which are valuable traits in the business world.

Listen

Listening is an essential trait to have in any business, especially as an accountancy or bookkeeping firm owner, because it helps you build strong relationships with your team, clients/customers, and partners. It enables you to make informed decisions based on feedback and insights. Here are three reasons why listening is vital in any business:

1. **Builds trust and rapport**: When you listen to others, it shows that you value their opinions and perspectives. This helps build trust and rapport, which is crucial for fostering strong relationships in business. This is especially important for an accountancy or bookkeeping firm as clients see you as an expert and someone they trust.

2. **Provides valuable insights**: Listening to feedback from team members, clients/customers, and partners can provide valuable insights into what is working well and what needs improvement. This information can help you make informed decisions and improve the overall success of the business.

3. **Promotes innovation**: Listening to diverse perspectives and ideas can promote innovation by providing fresh ideas and approaches to problem-solving. This has been so useful to me.

Be aware that most people when in conversation will be thinking of what they want to say in replying to what the person is saying instead of really listening to the person and asking questions to get more information or just to hear the full story. You miss out if you only look to reply with your own story and some people call this a 'story topper' i.e., my story is better than yours... I used to always do this and I had to consciously stop myself. I now write down what I want to bring up if I think it is important in a business setting otherwise, I will forget as I will be asking further questions and letting the person tell me everything before I go back to what I may want to say. If you are a 'topper' then be aware that you are and try to keep yourself in check.

This quote highlights this:

> "Most people do not listen with the intent to understand;
>
> they listen with the intent to reply."
>
> *Stephen Covey*

Listening is important as a means of effective communication and influence, understanding, and building relationships. As the accountancy or bookkeeping firm owner, listening can help you create a positive and productive work environment, make informed decisions, and ultimately drive the success of the business.

> "The art of conversation lies in listening."
>
> *Malcolm Forbes*

Self-Development

As a leader, continuous self-development is crucial for several reasons. First and foremost, it helps you stay relevant and adapt to the ever-changing business landscape. It also helps you stay engaged and motivated, sets a good example for your team, and allows you to improve your skills and knowledge. This leads to better decision-making and performance. It also helps you create the accountancy or bookkeeping firm's Vision.

Here are five reasons why continuous self-development is important for you as a leader:

1. **Keeps you relevant**: As a leader, it is important to keep up with the latest trends and best practices in your industry. Continuous self-development helps you stay relevant and ensures that you can lead your team effectively.

2. **Increases your knowledge and expertise**: Self-development helps you gain new knowledge and skills that can help you become a better leader. By continuously learning and improving, you can enhance your expertise and provide better guidance to your team.

3. **Boosts your confidence**: When you continuously self-develop, you gain a sense of confidence and self-assurance. This confidence can help you make better decisions and inspire your team to follow your lead.

4. **Helps you build a stronger team**: As you develop your leadership skills, you'll be better equipped to build a strong and cohesive team. You'll be able to identify your team member's strengths and weaknesses and provide the support they need to succeed.

5. **Encourages innovation and creativity**: Self-development can help you become more innovative and creative in your leadership approach. By

exploring new ideas and ways of doing things, you can inspire your team to think outside the box and come up with new and innovative solutions to problems.

Self-development helps you as a leader to develop the skills and mindset needed to adapt to change and overcome challenges. Always pursue self-development however you digest it, whether by reading, listening, watching or attending courses, talks, workshops etc. There is a lot of material out there which is free like podcasts, TED talks and YouTube videos. There is also a wide selection of self-improvement books available through Kindle, Audible and Blinkist. Plus, there are many good old face-to-face self-improvement events in the form of workshops, seminars, conferences and mastermind groups.

I am always listening to audiobooks, podcasts and YouTube programmes about business, leadership, management and more. Your smartphone is amazing and you can harness it to help you self-develop and listen to educational items whilst you are doing daily chores, walking the dog, exercising, driving, gardening or whatever. Invest in some good headphones that you can easily carry around with you and you can learn anywhere!

I find Blinkist, Audible, Kindle, YouTube and podcasts very useful for my self-development as well as accounting conferences and my mastermind group. The amazing thing with YouTube is you can listen and of course see the old greats in person like Napoleon Hill, Jim Rohn, Earl Nightingale, Stephen Covey and others who have passed away. Plus, you have those still with us like Brian Tracey, John Maxwell, Simon Sinek, Shawn Acher, Tony Robbins, Robert Greene and others.

The great thing is, you can hear exactly what they say, how they say it and feel a closer connection to their message which could only be improved on if you were in the room with them.

I subscribe to YouTube so I do not need to listen to adverts. I tend to listen to them on my phone rather than watch them, so I can do other things at the same time, that do not require too much focus like driving, chores around the house and gardening.

"Leadership and learning are indispensable to each other."

John F. Kennedy

Be a Great Leader!

Being a great leader is something I aspire to be and I think that if we are in a leadership position, we should always be considering how we can be better.

To be a great leader one must possess or develop a combination of skills and traits that inspire and guide your team towards success. A great leader is someone who not only has a clear vision but also effectively communicates and motivates others to achieve their goals.

Here are some essential qualities and tips on how to be a great leader. Some of these we have discussed in detail already and this brings them all together:

1. **Vision**: A great leader has a clear vision for the future and inspires others to work towards that vision.

2. **Communication**: Good communication skills are essential for any leader. The ability to articulate ideas and goals clearly, listen actively, and provide feedback effectively are key to building strong relationships with team members **(See the Chapter on Rhythm of the Business)**. This creates the environment and tools to aid communication.

3. **Empathy**: A great leader understands the needs and feelings of others and can empathise with them. This allows the leader to create a positive work environment where team members feel valued and motivated.

4. **Adaptability**: The ability to adapt to changing circumstances is critical for a leader. Great leaders can pivot quickly and make decisions in a dynamic and fast-paced environment

5. **Accountability**: A great leader takes responsibility for their actions and decisions and is willing to admit when they are wrong. This builds trust and respect among team members.

6. **Courage**: Leaders must have the courage to take risks and make difficult decisions, even when faced with uncertainty or opposition.

7. **Continuous Learning**: A great leader is always seeking to learn and improve, both personally and professionally. This allows the leader to stay ahead of the curve and lead with confidence.

> *"The greatest leader is not necessarily the one who does the greatest things.*
>
> *He (or she) is the one that gets the people to do the greatest things."*
>
> *Ronald Reagan*

Chapter 2

TEAM

2. TEAM

Build an A-Team

I loved the 'A-Team' as a kid and the music is always in my head. When I think about the TV series I always remember an angry BA saying, "You fool Murdock!"

Everyone had their role in that team and special skills and together they were the A-Team who could do anything, build anything and get the job done. Hannibal was the leader and ensured everyone was doing the right thing to make their adventure a success. As the business owner, you are Hannibal, the cigar-chewing leader and you have your specialist team around you who must do what they are good at and are assigned to do to ensure the job is done.

Have you got your A-Team around you? Are your team doing what they are best at?

Make sure you know what you want your A-Team to do and how many people you need.

Create an **Avatar** for each team member you want in your A-Team. You should do this if you want to hire a new person or promote from within, but you can also do this if you already have a team to ensure all are in the correct role.

An **Avatar** is a list of everything you want the person in a particular role to do and your ideal profile of that person. Remember you will never find the perfect fit; you want someone who can grow and develop and move forward with your business. The key is having someone in your A-Team who has a great attitude, with the capability and understanding of what is required of
53

them in the role and who knows their weak areas of knowledge and understands where they must develop.

The development will be through your mentoring and their self-learning. Mentoring could take place through others also, however what you want is proactive team members who are capable of self-learning. The mindset of a person in your A-Team is key as you cannot train this. They must of course fit your core values which we will talk about later.

Our Intelligent Outsourcing A-Team. Photo taken at a team building event in the Philippines in May 2023.

Write a **Letter of Expectation** of what you require of a person in their role. This is everything that you want to see from them.

For example – having a respectful attitude to other team members; how they should dress (e.g. casual smart; shirt and tie); personal hygiene; punctuality; speak to clients once a month; meet clients at least once a year in an annual accounts review meeting; not be drunk or high at work; work in the office at least three days per week; be active in team meetings; answer emails within

24 hours; if sick let the team know by 9.30 am; book holidays at least seven days in advance; always ensure someone can cover their work if they are on holiday; answer phone calls within four rings; study ACCA; carry out at least four hours of self-learning per month; if they have an issue bring it up within 24 hours; and if they need to discipline a subordinate do so within 24 hours.

It is worth **profiling your team** as this helps ensure your A-Team works most effectively together. It allows you all to gain a deep understanding of each team member's skills, strengths, weaknesses, and personalities. Profiling can be done through various means, such as assessments, surveys, and feedback sessions. There are many profiling tools; some of the most popular are DiSC, Strength Finder, Myers-Briggs, and Belbin.

Here are some reasons and benefits of profiling your team:

1.   **Improved communication**: Profiling can help team members understand each other's communication styles and preferences. This knowledge can reduce misunderstandings and conflicts, leading to improved communication.

2.   **Enhanced team performance**: Profiling can help team members recognise their strengths and weaknesses, allowing them to work on improving their skills. This can enhance team performance as each member can contribute their best.

3.   **Better team dynamics**: Profiling can help identify conflicts or tensions between team members. This knowledge can be used to address these issues and foster better team dynamics.

4. **Effective project assignment**: Profiling can help team leaders understand each member's skills and strengths, enabling them to assign projects that suit their individual abilities. This can increase project efficiency and productivity.

5. **Personal development**: Profiling can give team members valuable feedback about their skills and personality traits. This knowledge can help individuals work on personal development, enhancing their overall performance and job satisfaction.

6. **Increased team member retention**: Profiling can help managers identify team members' strengths and interests, allowing them to create development plans that align with the team member's goals. This can lead to increased job satisfaction and team member retention.

Profiling your team effectively enhances communication, team performance, and individual development, leading to a more productive and satisfied team.

"The strength of the team is each individual member.

The strength of each member is the team."

Phil Jackson

Simple Steps to Get Your A-Team:

1. Ensure each team member agrees with the **core values** of your business.

2. Make sure they **understand what is required** in the role. This is where a Letter of Expectation is handy to go through with them (**See Letter of Expectation**). Ask them for feedback on the role and ask how they would do it. This is to see if they 'get' what they need to do before they start the role. Unfortunately, you cannot be 100% sure until they perform the role.

3. They must be **capable** of doing the role. The person must be able to carry out their assignments correctly. This doesn't mean that they must already have done that type of role, but they must be someone who will develop and learn and who is capable of growing into the role.

   I have had many team members who have never done the role that I ask them to step into, and it would have been a steep learning curve for them. I was happy for them to take on the role as I knew they could learn, develop and ensure they do a great job. Yes, there will be mistakes on the way, which is all part of the learning process.

   If they cannot do what the role entails and never will be able to develop the skills to do the role, then you do not want them, at least in that role. Again, you may not know if they are capable of performing the role until they start it.

4. They **want the role and want to grow** to be good at the role. Attitude is a massive thing I always look for in any team member. If they have the right attitude, are keen to develop and learn and want to be part of the A-Team, then they are a great choice. Some people say that, "You only need a great attitude." This is incorrect. A great attitude minus an understanding of what is needed and the capability to do the role will

simply never work. You need the team member to have all three to take up an A-Team spot. Not forgetting that they must follow your core values. (**See Core Values**).

Our A-Team at Intelligent Outsourcing with #hamster

Core Values

Having core values for any business is critical to ensure everyone knows what behaviour is expected of them. It should be used when hiring to ensure all candidates for a role are aware of the core values and agree to them before joining. It should also be used in disciplinary situations, where you indicate how the core values have been breached.

If you do not have core values written down and publicly known, this does not mean you and your business do not have them. It just means that you have not articulated them.

It would be best if you did a workshop to come up with your core values. Book in time with your team and write things on a board until you end up with a list of core values you like. Then bring it down to three to seven. The less, the better and make sure the core value are easily remembered by all. You can create an acronym for the core values so you and your team remember them.

For example.

Naylor Accountancy Services has five core values, **iCARE**:

iNtegrity

Care

Accountability

Respect

Excellence

Intelligent Outsourcing has seven core values, **iCHARGE** – as in charging a battery, being in charge and charging forward with growth.

iNtegrity

Care

Have fun

Accountability

Respect

Growth

Excellence

Our office wall with core values clearly displayed.

Asda has four core values:

a. **Service** to our customers.

b. **Respect** for the individual.

c. Strive for **excellence**.

d. Act with **integrity.**

> *"Your values become your destiny."*
>
> Mahatma Gandhi

Letter of Expectation

A Letter of Expectation is basically what it says, a document stating precisely what you require from a team member in the position they hold addressed to them personally, hence a letter.

It can be used in two ways. One for an existing team member who is not fulfilling your expectations. Once your expectations are written down on paper, it makes it clear to you and your team member what is required to meet your expectations. Once you have gone through it with the team member, give them the physical Letter so they understand it. You should finish by asking them, "Do you agree with these expectations?" I would also say, "If you go away and have any queries about this, let me know."

If you do not want to give your Letter of Expectation to the team member as you fear they will take it personally and may leave, then you should still write it for your benefit. However, instead of giving them the Letter, have conversations with them around what you expect and get their buy-in and agreement.

While you may not give them the Letter of Expectation it is necessary to write it so you are clear about what you want from them in their role. By not giving them the Letter, you are ensuring you do not make things worse for yourself and the firm as some people have egos that are unable to deal with this type of feedback.

It can also be used when hiring a new team member. You create a Letter of Expectation which includes what you need the new team member to do. This is different to a job description as it is more in-depth. The Letter is how you want to see the team member behave, act and interact with people and more, as well as covering the actual role. We use this when hiring someone new and ensure the candidate agrees with our requirements before making an offer.

> ### Story of a Letter of Expectation.
>
> The first time I had to use a Letter of Expectation was for Gary who had just started with us. The team member sitting next to Gary complained that she could not be in the office with him as he was unkempt and smelt. The other team member stated that Gary looked and smelt like a homeless person. Gary was a qualified senior accountant who was good at his job.
>
> I had to do something quickly as there was an issue, and Gary would also be meeting with clients, so not a great ambassador for our accountancy firm despite him being a great accountant. When I interviewed Gary and subsequently met him for lunch, he had not exhibited any of these issues. He was clean, smart and presentable.
>
> I created a Letter of Expectation stating, amongst other things:
>
> You are required to be smart and presentable for work which includes:
>
> - Haircut and beard trim at least every six weeks;
> - Have a clean, ironed shirt every day;
> - Wear clean clothes that do not carry an unpleasant odour in the office;
> - Wear clothes that fit properly;

- Always have clean hair; and

- Ensure hair is clean-cut and smart and representative of a professional person. I can share some examples of what I mean by this if required.

I ended the letter by stating: I would like to support you with each of these points. If any matter requires further clarification, please let me know by return, and I will gladly assist. Any further breaches of the values or standards will result in disciplinary proceedings commencing. I trust this will not be necessary.

Yours Faithfully....

I went through the letter with Gary and he took it all onboard, making the changes required to meet the expectations. It was a matter of explaining to him what was required as he was oblivious to the issue as that was just how he had been for years.

Team NOT Employees or Staff

Do you currently use 'staff' or 'employee' when you talk about or with your accountancy team?

If so, I challenge you to make this simple change and use 'Team,' 'Team Member', and 'Our Team' when talking to clients, your team, friends and other accountants or anyone else. You will initially keep using the old term but keep going and make sure you catch yourself when you use the words staff or employee about your team.

I have to admit you still need to use the HMRC and accountancy terms when required, like 'employee benefits', 'employee NI', etc, so you cannot do away with these words completely.

So, always use the term Team, Team Member and Our Team (not 'your' or 'my' team if you can help it) as you could never do what you do without the Team. They know they are all part of the same team and are not your minions.

I have always done this in my UK accountancy firm, and all the team use it for each other too. I also use it in Intelligent Outsourcing although I had to train the team to use 'team' and not employee or staff. Now it is natural.

Richard Branson uses the term **teams** because he knows he can't do it by himself. That is the same for all of us.

Recruitment and Retention

Recruitment and retention of your team is the hardest thing to do. There are loads of books written by gurus on recruitment and retention. The key to retention is that you get the right people the first time who buy into your Vision and core values.

You will always have team members leaving, as you never know what is happening in their lives or heads. You must not beat yourself up and get straight on recruiting a replacement.

You must:

- Know what you want by creating the Avatar, as previously mentioned.
- Always ask for feedback from those leaving so you know what drove them to depart and if there are any changes you need to implement. Be aware that the leaver may not be telling you the truth, but there is always lessons to be learned from someone leaving.

Recruiting is currently a massive problem for accountancy or bookkeeping firms with very few candidates and the salaries of good accountants have skyrocketed. From speaking to many accountancy and bookkeeping firm owners, they say accountants in the UK can earn far more in commerce and industry and the work is less stressful, so they are opting to move out of accountancy firms. This creates a big issue! Who will you get and how will the work be done?

I had the same issue when I was growing my accountancy practice. I wanted to ensure an excellent service and I was struggling to offer it as getting good accountants who wanted to work for a small accountancy firm on a salary I could afford (my firm is in Tunbridge Wells so I was competing with London salaries) was very difficult. That is what drove me to create an offshore team in the Philippines and create Intelligent Outsourcing with the help of the local knowledge of Dee Smith and Christine Sy. We then developed the iO Academy to ensure all accountants were trained to a certain level and were continually developing to provide excellent service.

If you are struggling to get the team you want to do compliance work or bookkeeping, you should consider creating an offshore team. They are great at doing the compliance work and could be a good fit for your accountancy or bookkeeping firm.

You would want them to use all your processes and systems so you are in control. At the same time, you want to partner with an offshore company that cares about making it work for you and has the UK accountancy knowledge and training support you will need. **(See Core Values).** Then your UK team can focus on the client relationships and added value work.

See the Chapter on **Offshoring Team** to learn more.

Create a Leadership Team

Within your A-Team, you need people you can talk with on the same level about issues, strategy and vision. This is your Leadership Team. The team may be small to start with as you do not have a big enough business or the right people to be on it.

Ensure your Leadership Team grows as the business grows as you want 'buy-in' for the direction and decisions of the firm from those doing the work and managing others. You want all the hats of the business to be covered by your leadership team and people can wear more than one hat, which will be the case at the start.

As a business owner, you wear all the hats at the start of your business unless you have a business partner. If you do not have anyone to be on the leadership team with you it is advisable to build a Mastermind Group with others who have accounting practices of their own or better still join an established Mastermind Group like the Accountants Mastermind run by Simon Chaplin and Mark Swindale (I have been a member of this since 2016 and it has been invaluable to me).

When creating your Leadership Team, it is worth knowing exactly what you want from them and giving them clarity about this. You want them to highlight issues as you will not know everything, and the bigger you grow and/or get away from the doing the compliance work and client interactions, the more you will need to rely on the team to highlight issues.

You must have regular Leadership Team meetings. See the **'Regular Meetings'** section. This is key for them to feel empowered and you to feel secure that they have control of the business.

I have completely pulled away from all client relationships apart from some of my first clients with whom I have a strong relationship. I can sleep easily at night by leaving the Leadership Team with clear responsibilities and regular meetings with KPIs that ensure things stay on track. I have a great Leadership Team that can deal with the running of the business and issues. I am still in all the leadership meetings, so I can guide and be part of discussions of issues, after which we look at solutions and decide on the action(s) to take.

I have not abdicated responsibility for the business but delegated. I will step in and mentor and guide. Through regular meetings, I know what is happening, what the issues are and help in discussing and creating solutions for the issues. The key is that you cannot just turn your back on the business or you will lose it. Controls must be in place to ensure that everything functions as it should and that you are aware of issues before they escalate.

I know someone who recruited a Practice Manager to look after his business, allowing him to step back. However, the service levels dropped and they lost over half the business. He learned many lessons from that, and mine to you is to be aware of what is happening in the business without doing all the work – delegate but never abdicate responsibility. After all, if anything happens, you take ultimate responsibility and no one else!

> **"Alone we can do so little; together we can do so much."**
>
> *Helen Keller*

Our Intelligent Outsourcing Leadership Team at our Annual Way Forward Planning Meeting 2022 in the Philippines.

Chapter 3

RHYTHM OF THE BUSINESS

3. RHYTHM OF THE BUSINESS

It is critical that you create a regular rhythm for how your business is run and how communication happens. This comes through structuring and sticking to it. You want your team to work as one and be able to talk about issues they observe openly. The last thing you want is for a team member to feel that they have nothing to contribute and an issue they have raised has just been ignored.

The rhythm of managing any business is all about which meetings you have and how you communicate in them. This encompasses the regularity, time they take, who is involved in them and what is discussed.

Below is how we created our 'rhythm' in Naylor Accountancy Services and Intelligent Outsourcing. This approach is tried and tested, and although sometimes it may seem too much, when missed out on the odd occasion that it has, you notice it, and it effects the rhythm.

Following a regular rhythm is critical for your business. I describe below our meetings and how we run them. To start with, some team members thought this was too much, but now they all see their importance and hate to miss them when they are away.

I will start with the most frequent rhythm meeting and work up to the ones done annually.

Daily Huddle

This is where the team gets together every morning for 15 minutes tops and each person has one to two minutes to talk about what happened the previous day and what they are working on that day. If a team member needs a hand or has any queries, they will also mention them. This is the regular pulse for Naylor Accountancy Services as we have most of our accountants and two administrators in the Philippines with Intelligent Outsourcing, so we need the team in the UK and Philippines to feel like they are part of the same team. The daily huddle is held on a Teams video call; before that came into existence, it was via Skype.

Some people call it a 'daily scrum' and is something that used to happen in the IT programme development team when I worked in the City of London. It was done standing in a circle on the open floor to ensure it was quick. You can do regular weekly team huddles, but I would not recommend anything less frequent. It does help create the team atmosphere you want for any business.

Daily huddle with Naylor Accountancy Services – online.

Weekly Leadership Meetings

This is done on the same day and time each week; if people cannot make it, they just miss it, and the meeting continues. If you are away, you just have someone else run the meeting. It is typically 1.5 hours long, starts on time, and finishes on time.

In the meeting, you start with a few minutes with everyone sharing anything interesting they have done or will be doing personally. This is to get everyone engaged and help connect with each other.

Then go through your business data, anything that you want to measure for your business that will have an impact if you aren't moving in the required direction. For an accounting or bookkeeping firm, this could be:

1. Number of new clients signed up in the month;
2. Number of clients resigning;
3. Number of accounts completed in the month so far;
4. Number of Self-Assessments completed in the month so far;
5. Number of VAT Returns done after a specific internal deadline. This could be the 25th of the month;
6. Profit so far for the month;
7. Turnover for the month;
8. Debtors for the month; and
9. Whatever else you want to measure.

Then go through any **actions** that were created from the previous meeting. Every action created only has **ONE person responsible** for it, meaning there is nowhere to hide so, ask if it has been done or not.

Usually, an action should be completed within the week, but you can allow it to move over for another week but anything more than two weeks may be an issue, so you may need to discuss further.

Weekly Leadership Meeting with Intelligent Outsourcing in the Philippines office with two dialling in from the UK and Canada.

Issues – finally, establish the business's current issues and which is the most important one and then discuss the issue. The issue as it has been presented rarely is the real issue, so make sure everyone is drilling down into it and probing to understand all the factors relating to the one described.

Once you have established the real issue, you should all brainstorm potential solutions. You will then be able to decide the solution to the issue between your leadership team.

The solution becomes an 'action', and it is allocated to one of the leadership team to ensure it is carried out. They will report back on the action in the next weekly meeting.

Close the meeting on time. If you have not covered all the issues do not worry these will be covered in next week's meeting. If there is an urgent issue that needs to be resolved before the next meeting, then book a separate meeting to cover it that week.

1:1 Meetings

It is essential to have regular one-to-one (1:1) meetings with your direct reports. For you, this could be your entire team if you are a small firm or limited to those in your leadership team if you are larger firm. The leadership team would then have 1:1 meetings with their team, cascading down further if you are a large firm.

In these 1:1 meetings, you go through what they are working on led by them, what you see as necessary going forward, and any issues they have, and always ask them at the end of the meeting, **"Is there anything else?"** then pause. Do not break the silence as some team members take a while to think and build up the courage to say what is still on their mind.

Always ask this and train others to ask, "Is there anything else?" at the end of the meeting.

You can do 1:1s weekly, bi-weekly or monthly. I would not do less frequently than monthly, and you can vary the frequency depending on what is going on in your business and how comfortable you are leaving the team members to get on with things without your guidance or knowledge of what is happening.

Quarterly Review Meeting

These meetings provide everyone with a 90-day attention span to focus on a project. This is why the Quarterly Review Meeting is critical. In it you set the following quarterly projects and allocate each action point to an individual to ensure there is one person responsible for it. This means it will get done.

This meeting is a whole day. You may think, "We do not have enough to talk about for a full day." You will be surprised what comes up and by having a structure of the things you will cover in the meeting. We typically have ours starting at 9 am and finishing at 4 pm with an hour for lunch and everyone is exhausted at the end!

You can shorten it initially, but you will soon want the whole day. We did that initially and just overran. You do not want distractions from incoming calls, emails and other team members. You can ensure this by having the meeting out of the office.

We have our Naylor Accountancy Services Quarterly Review Meeting in the board room of our shared offices and turn all emails off and ensure our out-of-office emails are on and the rest of the team know to only disturb us if urgent. We have two people dial in on Teams as they are based in the Philippines and are in the Intelligent Outsourcing board room.

Review Previous Quarter

Start the Quarterly Review Meeting with positivity and have each person provide the following:

a) What do they think are the most significant three achievements of the business in the last 90 days?

b) Their greatest personal accomplishment; and

c) What they are expecting of the day.

Once this is complete, you go through **the quarterly KPIs** you are measuring, the goals and the financials, only stating if expectations were met. If they were not met, then there could be an issue to discuss, so have that written down to cover later in the meeting.

Then go through the **quarterly projects** set to get an update on whether they are completed. If not completed, then you need to decide on the following:

a) Carry forward;

b) Reassign to another person; or

c) If virtually completed, then move to the 'to do'.

Quarterly Review Meeting with the Naylor Accountancy Services Leadership Team in July 2023 with two dialling in from the Philippines and #hamster

Review the Way Forward Plan

This is the Vision the 10-year, 3-year and 1-year plan document created at the start of the year (See **Way Forward Plan**). It is vital that everyone still believes in this, and if any changes are needed due to circumstances changing, then this is the time to discuss them and agree on any changes. It also ensures everyone is reminded of the Way Forward Plan to sharpen the leadership teams focus on achieving what is expected.

Ensure you have a 10–15-minute pause after two hours, as people will need a comfort break.

Establish Next Quarter's Projects

You may already have some quarterly projects to carry forward, so add them to the list for the next quarter. Create a list of all that must be done in the next 90 days to meet your one-year plan and any new obligations.

Discuss the top three to eight projects you all want to work on in the next quarter. Be careful not to overload the team with projects as then nothing will get done. It is better to have fewer projects so the team can focus on them and complete them. You can then pick up the other projects in the next quarter.

Assign each quarterly project to a person. Again, this is to ensure it gets done as there is no one else responsible apart from that person. The person can delegate and get others to work on the project too, but it is their responsibility to ensure that the project is completed and no one else's.

The Quarterly Projects are created and must be documented with the person responsible for them.

Lunch – ensure you know when you want to break for lunch and when you get to that time then finish off any discussion you are in the middle of and break. Break for 45 minutes to an hour as you need to all eat and reflect.

Carry on where you broke off for lunch, you may have completed all the above already so just move on fitting within your timeframe.

Discuss key issues

Go through the list of issues you have for the business from the weekly meetings and that have been brought up from this quarterly meeting. If the new quarterly projects will be dealing with one of the issues, then remove it and then decide which are the top three issues.

Discuss the first top issue and establish if indeed the issue stated is the issue. Do dive down into the issue as it invariably is not the issue you need to deal with. Once you have talked over the issue, what it is, and how it impacts the business and people, then look at potential solutions. Everyone should participate and give their views to get good depth feedback into the issue and potential solutions. Nothing is a bad idea; everything should be discussed.

Once all solutions have been brought forward then decide what solution you all agree the business should take. Add this solution to the 'To-do list' and assign a person responsible for it.

Keep moving on to the next issue until you run out of issues or are 30 minutes near the end of the meeting. Then move into concluding the quarterly review.

Conclude

Confirm the projects for the next quarter and who is responsible for them and then do the same for projects or to-dos that have been noted and are still live.

Ensure these are written down and circulated after the meeting. If the Way Forward Plan has changed then a new edited document must be created and circulated to all.

Decide if a message needs to be given to the rest of the team on what you have decided in the meeting. If it does, ensure you communicate this message and it is always best done in person at a companywide meeting or town hall. If all the team are present in the quarterly review meeting, then this is unnecessary.

Ask all participants of the meeting if their expectations for the meeting were met. If not, ask for what specifically, why, and how they could ensure that their expectations are met next time.

Annual Way Forward Planning Meeting

This is a critical meeting that you must have with your leadership team, if you are too small to have a Leadership Team you can just do this meeting by yourself. The reason for having the Annual Way Forward Planning Meeting is for you to create a plan that encompasses your vision, build it out and create the steps you need to take to get to where you want to be. Ideally you will want to do this with your Leadership Team so they all buy into it and have a say in creating it.

This is important as without others wanting to carry the torch for the business you cannot grow the company. If you are the only person creating it that is fine, if you have a team you must share what you are happy sharing with them once you have created your Way Forward. This will help them understand what you are looking to achieve and why you are wanting to do what you have planned.

I did the Annual Way Forward Planning Meeting myself until I was in a position to create a Leadership Team for Naylor Accountancy Services. So, this is something you should do whatever size you are.

Allow two days for the Annual Way Forward Planning Meeting and this should ideally be somewhere where you are not disturbed, so out of the office is best. The key is not to be disturbed or distracted by the day-to-day operations of your accountancy or bookkeeping firm.

I will break down the meeting so you can see the structure of this meeting which is simple.

Day 1

Personal news – start lightly with all participants mentioning something that they have just done that was fun or of interest. This helps everyone to get to know each other better and ensures all have something to say at the start to get their talking juices flowing.

Personal review of last year

Each meeting participant needs to share the following:

- Three biggest accomplishments of the business in the last year;
- Personal accomplishments that mean the most in the last year; and
- Expectations for the Annual Way Forward Planning Meeting.

Review previous year

This will already have been formulated by the person who is responsible for the accountancy or bookkeeping firm KPIs and financials and typically runs through the following:

- Achievements of the year (what was already mentioned by individuals should be in this plus others);
- Goals that have been achieved;
- Financials – profits, debtors, cash, margin, etc;
- Non-financials – number of clients, team members, etc;
- KPIs – were they met or not? and
- Projects last quarter – completed or not?

Pause a couple of hours after the start of the meeting with a 10–15-minute comfort break and then pick up again.

SWOT analysis on the business

I am sure you are familiar with a SWOT analysis as you must have done many, but I will just highlight it and the reason for having to do one in your Annual Way Forward meeting.

SWOT analysis is a strategic planning tool used to evaluate a business strengths, weaknesses, opportunities, and threats. Here's a quick breakdown of each component:

- **Strengths:** Internal factors that give an advantage, such as expertise, resources, or a strong brand;
- **Weaknesses**: Internal factors that put the business at a disadvantage, such as poor management, lack of resources, or low team member morale;
- **Opportunities**: External factors that can benefit the business, such as new market trends, emerging technologies, or changes in consumer behaviour; and
- **Threats**: External factors can harm the business, such as increased competition, economic downturns, or regulatory changes.

SWOT analysis helps you make informed decisions and develop effective strategies by considering these four key elements.

By analysing these components, you can identify your competitive position and develop strategies to address areas of weakness and take advantage of opportunities. Add anything that comes up in the weakness to the issues list and potentially also some of the threats, but only if you can do anything about them or make the issue have less impact.

Doing a SWOT analysis every year is a must as it ensures the participation of everyone in the room, getting them to think about the business as a whole and helping get them on board with the creation of the Vision in the next steps.

SWOT Analysis written up on the walls in the Naylor Accountancy Services Annual Way Forward Planning Meeting.

Break for Lunch – do this whatever time you decide to have lunch and then pick up where you left off afterwards. Allow up to an hour.

10-year Vision

Discuss or think about (if just you) what you want this to look like. For example, total turnover, profit margin, profit, how many clients, how many offices, how many team members, and the average client fee. Put as much detail into this as possible.

This discussion is one of the most interesting if you have a Leadership Team. I have found that my 10-year Vision has been stretched further by the Leadership Team, as they can see we have a far more significant potential.

Target market – be clear about what types of clients you focus on. It does not mean you do not take on clients that do not fall into this category, it just gives you focus on who you're ideally looking to bring in.

For example:

     i)   Type of businesses you want – e.g. tech companies, building companies, retail, dentists, doctors, agencies, creatives, trades etc;

     ii)   Turnover of the companies you would like – e.g. £100k-£500k, £150k-£1m, £250k-£2m, or whatever you would like to target. Note: the larger the company, the longer they usually take to make decisions and often things change so it is a good idea to set an upper limit;

     iii)   Number of business owners of the clients you bring on – e.g., one business owner, three partners etc. It is easiest with one owner as there is only one main decision maker;

     iv)   Number of team members they have; and

     v)   Location of the businesses.

Confirm what your **Unique Selling Points** (USPs) are and look to keep this to three. This should incorporate your culture, belief and what you do. For example, you can highlight one of your core values (See the section on **Core Values**); how you operate through technology; types of meetings; help companies grow; niche etc.

Review what makes your accountancy or bookkeeping firm unique. This can be difficult to come up with so keep looking, as soon as you have three USPs you have it and it is easier to market and sell to clients.

Core values – check everyone is still in agreement with the core values. If not then debate this, as all must agree on the core values, and it may need some tweaking if there is a reason to make a change. If this is the case, educational communication will be needed to the rest of the team explaining the change and why.

Until the 10-year vision has been agreed by your Leadership Team you must continue to discus and debate it. This will inspire the leadership team as they will be committed to the Vision as they helped create it. This is dynamite and will mean full engagement moving forward.

This is precisely what I have experienced with my Leadership Team in Naylor Accountancy Services and Intelligent Outsourcing. They made the vision grander than I had initially created for both businesses.

Annual Way Forward Planning Meeting with leadership team of
Intelligent Outsourcing December 2022 in the Philippines with two
dialling in from UK and Canada

3-year Picture

Once you agree to your 10-year Vision, move onto the 3-year Picture. Create this picture together so the leadership team knows what it looks, smells and feels like. Get a clear picture with the date stated on what you expect in three year's time.

For example:

3 years from today's date:

Measurables

- Revenue
- Profit
- Margin
- Number of clients
- Average fee per client

What it looks like

- Number of offices and locations
- Number of team members
- Number of client managers
- Number of acquisitions
- Role you will have then
- Leadership team in place that is strong
- Number of potential client enquiries per month
- Part of a mastermind group
- What technology you will have in place
- Regular leadership meetings – Weekly, quarterly and annual

- All clients do an Annual Plan with us
- Offshoring team doing all the compliance work

1-year Plan

First, I would write a list of your business's issues. This will help you create the one-year plan, as some of the goals will be solutions to these issues.

With the 3-year Picture created, you can easily see what you need to do in the next 12 months. Again, this would have the measurables you want to achieve at the end of the year and the goals within the business you want to achieve over the 12 months.

For example:

1 year from today's date:

Measurables

- Revenue
- Profit
- Margin
- Number of clients
- Average fee per client

Goals for the year

- Credit control process in place
- Happiness survey sent to clients and team members
- KPIs implemented for every team member and a monthly meeting with the team to go through them
- Fee reviews all clients
- Acquisition

- Hire a new Client Manager
- Create an offshore team to do bookkeeping, VAT, payroll and year-end accounts

End Day 1 – you should end the day once you have been at it for six hours as you will be shattered but do not go over seven hours. We tend to do 9 am to 4 pm with breaks as mentioned.

Annual Way Forward Planning Meeting for Naylor Accountancy Services
February 2023 with two dialling in from the Philippines

Day 2

Pick up the second day where you left off the first day. You may have gone slower or quicker. The key is to just follow an agenda and keep to it, so you get everything done. You may need to discuss some areas for longer than others which is fine if you get everyone on the same page.

Establish the next quarter's projects.

Create a list of all that must be done in the next 90 days to continue meeting your one-year plan.

Discuss the top three to eight projects you want to work on in the next quarter. Refrain from overloading with projects, as then nothing will get done. It is better to have fewer so the team can focus on them and complete them. You can then pick up the other projects in the next quarter.

Assign each quarterly project to a person. Again, this is to ensure it gets done as no one else is responsible apart from that person. The person can delegate and get others to work on the project too, but it is their responsibility to ensure that the project is completed.

The Quarterly Projects are created and must be documented, each with a named project owner.

Break – schedule a 10-15 minute comfort break for two hours after the start time. This would usually be around 11.

Break for Lunch – do this at whatever time you decide to have lunch and then pick up where you left off afterwards. Allow up to an hour. This would typically be around 1pm.

Key issues discussed

Go through the list of issues you have, including those you added during your Annual Way Forward meeting. If the new quarterly projects will deal with one of the issues, remove it and then decide which are the top three issues.

Discuss the first top issue and establish if the issue stated is the real issue. Dive down into the issue as it invariably is different from the issue you need to deal with. Once you have discussed the issue, what it is, and how it impacts the business and people, look at potential solutions. Everyone should participate and give their views to provide in-depth feedback to the issue and possible solutions. Nothing is a bad idea; everything should be discussed.

Once all solutions have been discussed, you must collectively decide what solution the business should take. Add this solution to the 'to-do list' and assign a person responsible for it.

Keep doing this process, moving on to the next issue until you run out of issues or have only one hour remaining at which point you need to move into concluding the meeting.

Conclude

Confirm the projects for the next quarter and who is responsible. Then do the same for the 'to-dos' that were created and are not dealt with by one of the projects. Again, ensure the person responsible for dealing with them knows they are accountable.

All projects and to-dos must be written down and circulated after the meeting.

Talk through the Way Forward you have just created, highlighting the 10-year Vision, 3-year Picture and 1-year Plan. You want everyone to visualise what the accountancy or bookkeeping firm will look like if you all follow the agreed steps.

Decide what message needs to be given to the rest of the team about the Way Forward you have just created or updated. Ensure you communicate this and it is always best done in person in a companywide meeting or town hall or personally by the leadership team to their direct reports.

If all the team are present in the Annual Way Forward Planning meeting, then this is unnecessary.

Ask all participants of the meeting for feedback on the meeting and if their expectations for the meeting were met. If not, ask why and how you could ensure their expectations are met next time.

You always want to ask how a meeting went and if it did not go, then you want to know how to make the meetings better next time, so always ask for feedback.

Rules of a Meeting

I have done so many meetings. The one thing I hate is when I have a meeting and the only person engaged is me. Have you ever had that happen?

There is no point in having a meeting if others are not participating and sharing their thoughts and experiences. You may as well just allocate jobs with no meeting or discussion. Some business owners do run their firm like this, but they are missing out on new ideas, innovations, finding out what is really going on etc.

The reason for creating a leadership team is that you want them to be able to think independently so they can act without you having to constantly tell them what to do next. You especially want them to tell you when something is not going well so you can all discuss what should be done.

If a team member just continues doing what you have told them despite knowing it is wrong, nothing will be achieved. Then everyone is wasting their time and it will end up costing you and the business money and wasted time.

A team member may do this as they may think that they cannot say anything to you as you are the boss. It is far better for you to be happy to be challenged on a decision and for the team member to be happy to challenge and query what they are being asked to do. However, it does not mean that you will change anything you had planned to do if you still believe your planned action is the correct one.

The difference in allowing a conversation on why the team member believes another action is better than the one you had planned is that you have listened to their reasoning, thought about it, and then explained your reasoning to carry on with your course of action.

When I start a team meeting, especially the Weekly, Quarterly Review and the Annual Way Forward Meeting, I start it with the following reminder of what I am expecting from them in the meeting with the acronym **PHOOD** with an 'F' for 'ph' so it is **'FOOD' for thought before you start the meeting.**

- **Participation** – all must be 100% taking part in the meeting with discussions. This means no work emails, messaging or taking calls. Everyone must be focussed on the meeting as we want to hear all perspectives.
- **Have fun** – one thing we look to do is have fun at work, which does not mean that the team are having fun all the time and not focusing on work. It means we want them to enjoy being at work and are happy being at work as we spend most of our week at work.
- **Optimism** – do not take a doom and gloom scenario as your default, instead think all can be done with a plan in place and steps to execute it.
- **Ownership** – take ownership of your actions and your responsibilities. Do not blame others or make excuses.
- **Do not think you know everything** – it is vital you **listen** to others and be open to hearing what others say, so do not make your mind up before you hear other points of view.

Chapter 4

BUSINESS

STRUCTURE

4. BUSINESS STRUCTURE

Create Systems and Procedures

It is important to define what a system is as this highlights its importance. **A business system is a set of principles, practices and procedures applied to specific activities to achieve a specific result.**

Within an accountancy or bookkeeping firm, most of what is done is the same thing being done repeatedly. Therefore, you want to ensure that everyone is doing their jobs consistently to the standard you want. The only way you can ensure this is to create systems and procedures that the team must follow when they do a job like a VAT Return, Year-End Accounts, Self-Assessment or onboarding a new client.

These systems and procedures must be written up and then improved while ensuring everyone is aware of improvements to the procedures. Everyone in the team who needs to do the procedure must have access to the write-up. You can use process management software to write up all procedures like SweetProcess, but Microsoft Word works well.

Systems and procedures are critical components of any business as they provide **structure, consistency, and clarity in operations**. By defining and documenting procedures, a business can ensure that all team members understand their roles and responsibilities and how to perform their tasks effectively and efficiently.

One of the primary benefits of having well-defined systems and procedures is that they help create a consistent service quality level. By following a set of established steps, team members can deliver the same level of quality regardless of who is performing the task. This consistency is essential for building a reputation for excellent service, which can lead to increased client/customer satisfaction and loyalty.

Another advantage of having systems and procedures in place is that they can help to minimise errors, mistakes, and accidents. By outlining the steps needed to perform a task correctly, potential problems can be identified and addressed before they occur. Additionally, by documenting the steps, team members can refer back to the procedures if they need help with how to perform a task, reducing the likelihood of errors or mistakes.

Having written procedures in place ensures that all team members are on the same page and clearly understand what is expected of them. This can help prevent misunderstandings or confusion, particularly when multiple team members are involved in completing a task. It also stops everyone from doing their job differently and missing out on steps.

Finally, **it is essential to update systems and procedures when issues or mistakes occur.** This allows you and the team to learn from mistakes and prevent them from happening again. You can become more efficient, effective, and successful by continuously improving processes and procedures.

We have our ongoing 'Project Perfect' in Naylor Accountancy Services. Whenever a mistake happens, we add it to our Project Perfect list and we discuss the issue in our weekly meeting to come up with a solution as to what we can do to prevent it from happening again. We then update the relevant procedures for the job and let the team know of the change.

There are many different systems that you should have procedures written up for. You can use technology to help with many of these to ensure constancy, speed and ability to delegate. Here are a few examples of the systems for accountancy and bookkeeping firms:

- Onboarding a new client system;
- Pricing system – GoProposal software can help with this and other pricing systems;
- Sales system;
- Debtors' system;
- Billing system;
- Workflow system;
- KPI system;
- Client/customer service system;
- Year-end accounts system;
- VAT production system;
- Self-assessment system;
- Management accounts system; and
- Payroll and CIS system.

Each of the systems above could have a book written about them independently. The **two books on systems I recommend** you read are:

1. ***Banish the Bottleneck****: 7 savvy steps to grow the (almost) perfect team for your accountancy practice* by Simon Chaplin, as this gives loads of ideas for KPI systems.

2. ***Selling To Serve***: *The Breakthrough Sales System For Accountants* by James Ashford as this is great for Sales Systems.

Both these books are a must-read for accountancy and bookkeeping firm owners.

You may be concerned that you must write down all the procedures but that is not the case. You should get your team to record them up and then you can review them. The key is to have this in writing so it can be improved upon as required. When we are training someone new on a procedure they will go through the written procedure, update it and improve it if required.

Ideally, you want to have the systems run the business and the team run the systems. The result is that anyone can take over the job if someone leaves and you can retain the desired level of service.

> *"Great systems and procedures are the backbone of any successful business."*
>
> Peter Drucker

Organisational Structure and Functions

Any business must have an organisational structure with functions being carried out by various team members and this is no different for accounting or bookkeeping firms.

As a business owner, you are initially likely to carry out all the functions of your organisation. It is worth being aware of the different functions so that you can look to pass on the responsibilities for functions as you grow and have team members who can take them on, or you are able to outsource some functions. In either case, the ultimate responsibility must lie within your business.

There are effectively 10 different functions or departments that any business has, and you are probably doing most of these. However, you should delegate responsibility for the various functions where possible. (See Chapter on **Delegation**).

<u>The 10 Functions of Your Business</u>

1. Shareholder
2. Director/Visionary
3. Primary Leader
4. Service/Product Development
5. Operations
6. Marketing
7. Sales
8. Finance
9. HR
10. Admin/IT

You can only have one primary leader of the business, and only one person can be responsible for a function, but one person can have more than one function under them. Having a function responsibility does not mean that you have to do all the work as you will no doubt have people to delegate to. Still, you are ultimately responsible for the tasks under that function, and you must ensure that projects and tasks under that function are carried out and not blame anyone but yourself if not.

Structure of 10 Functions in Relation to Each Other

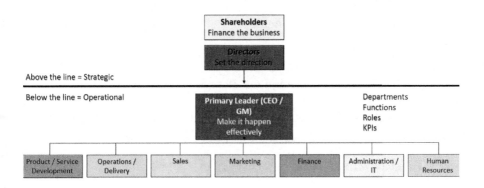

- The strategic nature of the business is the Shareholders and Directors who create the vision and direction of your business. You are sitting with these functions, and you should have your Leadership Team involved in creating the vision that sets the trend. See **Annual Way Forward Meeting** in the Chapter on **Rhythm of the Business.**

The rest of the functions are operational, with the primary leader being the one leader of the business in charge of making the vision happen. This is typically a CEO or General Manager in a large organisation and more than likely you.

This is the function that you ultimately want to delegate to someone else if you want to have others run your firm while you focus on the strategy and other ways of spending your time such as with the family, on the golf course etc..

However, this is not something we all want to achieve, and you may enjoy being the primary leader and doing the strategic work. As mentioned, one can have more than one function and typically, a business owner will have all the functions at the start of the business.

Each function has different responsibilities, and although the names are self-explanatory, you should ensure the roles of each are specified. This is why each task or project created is allocated to one person and should be the person under that function. See the Chapter on **Rhythm of the Business** as this describes how this works in practice.

The key responsibilities of each function must be clear and written down along with tasks. Take a look at the **Chapter on Team** which talks about ensuring a clear job description with expectations, priorities, etc.

By writing out the key responsibilities of each function, you ensure that no area is neglected. If all the functions are with you, then should delegate what you can. Do empower others to take on the responsibilities of that function and be careful not to inadvertently take it back. Mentor the person and allow them to make mistakes as long as they keep moving forward and learning from the mistakes.

Create an organisational chart with the people responsible for each function marked on the chart so all know who is taking on the function responsibility. Initially, you have to take on most of the functions. This allows you to identify what you should delegate as you grow the business. It also clarifies to others and you who is responsible for a specific function.

> "Organisations which design systems that are effective are those that are able to attract and retain the best employees."
>
> *W. Edwards Deming*

Agendas

Agendas are essential for meetings because they provide a structure and a roadmap for the discussion that will take place. Without an agenda, meetings can become disorganised, unfocused, and unproductive. I have done too many without an agenda, thinking I have it all in my head only to forget to go through one of the things I wanted to. Worse is someone calls a meeting with me and they have no agenda on what they want to talk through, and we waste time talking about things that are not important.

Here are some specific reasons why agendas are important for meetings:

1. **Help participants prepare**: An agenda allows attendees to prepare for the meeting by knowing the topics to be discussed, the goals to be achieved, and any information they need to bring.

2. **Keep meetings on track**: An agenda sets the framework for the meeting and helps keep discussions focused on the topics at hand. This can prevent the meeting from going off-topic, getting side-tracked, or going over time.

3. **Ensure that important topics are addressed**: By outlining the key points to be discussed, an agenda ensures that important topics are not overlooked or forgotten.

4. **Facilitate participation**: When attendees know what will be discussed, they are more likely to participate actively and contribute meaningfully to the meeting.

5. **Provide a record of the meeting**: Agendas can be used to document what was discussed and form the basis of meeting minutes as easy to add the decisions made, and action items assigned, which can be used as a reference for future meetings or to track progress on action items.

You will see in the Chapter **Rhythm of the Business** that there is a structure to them with an agenda. The one that is more off-piste is the 1:1 meeting as it is not specific and can be just a chat to see how everything is going for the team member.

Overall, agendas are essential for meetings because they help ensure the meeting is productive, efficient, and achieves its objectives.

> "An agenda clarifies the purpose of the meeting and what you want to accomplish."
>
> *Harvey Mackay*

Chapter 5

OFFSHORING TEAM

and

OUTSOURCING

5. OFFSHORING TEAM and OUTSOURCING

I will start by defining 'offshoring' as it can be confusing. Offshoring is a subset of outsourcing, so it is easy to get mixed up. As an accountancy or bookkeeping firm you have two choices if you are looking to bring in external help to get your compliance work done. You can either:

1. **Outsource the work** to a third party using their systems and procedures. You have to give them the work in a specific format and then receive it back for review. The person will likely be different each time, so they will not know the clients or how you want things done.

2. **Offshore the work with a team exclusively working for you** using your systems and processes. Your offshore team will get to know your clients and learn how you want things done. Your offshore team must be integrated into your existing team, so they feel part of your team.

Creating your offshore team, in my opinion, is far more effective so it is an intelligent way to outsource work for any accountancy or bookkeeping firm. Offshoring is where you have someone who works for you in another country that is more cost-effective and where the supply of accountants is better than in the home country.

You can get a **FREE Whitepaper** of in-depth independent analysis on offshoring for accountants if you go to the www.intelligentoutsourcing.co.uk website.

An offshore team uses all your accountancy or bookkeeping firm's systems and processes and the team works solely for your firm as part of your

113

accountancy team. Your offshore team must be integrated with your existing team.

One way that you can create the space and time to be able to focus on added value work, grow your business and do the things you want to do is by creating an offshore team. This is what I did with **Naylor Accountancy Services**.

I was struggling to get local accountants to join the accountancy firm, and at the start, I needed more profit to warrant paying for a fully qualified accountant with experience. Creating an offshore team meant that I could get all the compliance and bookkeeping done by others who were also able to source the data and information directly from the clients. This saved me further time as I did not need to email clients asking questions or chasing for information or documents. Emails take up so much time, as I am sure they do for you too.

Naylor Accountancy Services offshore team dinner

in the Philippines, May 2023.

The key difference between offshoring and outsourcing is that your offshore team develops and grows. They learn from their mistakes. They build relationships with your clients. They are interested in the success of your firm and want to develop with your business.

I started with my offshore team just doing bookkeeping and then moved to VAT, Payroll, and Year-end Accounts. Finally, we got them to do Self-assessments and Management Accounts. The offshore team used and developed my Naylor Accountancy Services systems and processes and all my accounting software. The offshore team has been integral in improving the procedures and systems and writing the updated procedures.

Intelligent Outsourcing Accountants in our office in the Philippines.

As well as my accountancy firm, I have **Intelligent Outsourcing Ltd,** and we find that many of our accountancy firm partners start with bookkeeping and

VAT on their first offshore team member(s) and then grow the team and capacity to take on Payroll, Year-end Accounts and Management Accounts.

We have one very prominent and successful accountancy firm that started their offshore accounting team with Intelligent Outsourcing. Their offshore-team consists of experienced accountants doing high-value work, management reporting and analysis and year-end accounts only. The firm now has seven offshore team members with us and has recommended us to many others.

We have another sizeable prominent accountancy practice that only started in July 2022. They had five offshore team members with Intelligent Outsourcing within five months and are still growing their offshore team.

We also have small firms that just need one person to take on compliance and bookkeeping tasks from them so that the UK team or the firm owner can focus on growing their accountancy or bookkeeping firm. If they carried on doing the compliance work themselves, then they would never grow the business. An offshore team member provides them with someone they can rely on to do the work and communicate directly with their clients. The business owner saves themselves time while increasing the service to their clients as the offshore team member will respond to the email quicker.

Requesting or chasing for information or documents takes up so much time for all accountants and holds up compliance work. So, having an offshore team that can do this as part of their job saves your UK team time which they can use to focus on client-added value, meetings, tax planning, new client generation, upselling or whatever else you want them to do that has a higher value.

The Offshore Team of Intelligent Outsourcing in the Philippines 2022

For Naylor Accountancy Services, I have my offshore team connect and talk directly to clients, and we have done special vocal coaching with the admin team members who answer the phone for the firm.

Once you have an offshore team that is growing, I would suggest you consider adding an admin person. This helps with requesting and chasing for information and documents rather than the accountants always having to do this. This way the accountants can concentrate on the compliance work that they are skilled to do. There are loads of tasks that an admin person can do for your firm. Here are a few examples:

Admin work:
- o Email clients requesting information for the Year-end Accounts;
- o Email clients requesting documents for their Self-assessment Return;
- o Email clients requesting the documents needed to set up a Limited Company;

- Continue emailing clients for information already requested until they receive it;
- Call clients asking when they can expect information or documents when email chasing has been ignored;
- Set up Limited Companies and send information to clients once done;
- Onboard clients, sending out emails requesting information and documents;
- Set up all jobs for new work orders or new clients on the practice management system;
- Update all KPI data required;
- Check that all work has been invoiced;
- Review client fees and discuss with the relevant person if the fee needs to change;
- Ad hoc work;
- Company Secretariate work – change address with HMRC and Companies House, add new directors along with all documentation signed by clients, new shareholding set up and create documents for signing and file; change in directors; change in the company name; etc; and
- Answers your phone and deals with enquiries or directs the calls appropriately.

Benefits of creating an offshore team:

1. Attract and retain talented accountants;

2. Costs considerably less than employing their UK equivalent;

3. Someone else deals with HR;

4. They use your systems and processes; and

5. They do the work you want them to do to the required standard.

The key to making offshoring work:

1. Make the offshore team feel part of your whole firm;

2. Make sure all your existing team are happy about you having offshore team members;

3. Regular team meeting with all – daily huddles or weekly or monthly meetings at the very least;

4. Train your offshore team well in your systems and processes;

5. Have them work in an office, not from home;

6. Immediately let your offshore partner know if there are any issues so they can quickly rectify them; and

7. Commit to offshoring.

There is a lot more that can be said about offshoring and how to make it a success. If you want to find out more, you can come to one of my regular webinars or go to www.intelligentoutsourcing.co.uk where there is loads of material for you to look at including videos, testimonials and, as mentioned early, a free Whitepaper entitled *The Proven Benefits of Offshoring Accountancy*.

Also visit our website if you want to hear what others say about offshoring and how we make it work with the well-respected **iO Academy** at the heart of everything.

The Intelligent Outsourcing accounting team in one of our offices in the Philippines with #hamster

Summary

Summary

You should now be aware of all that will ensure you have an ineffective accountancy or bookkeeping firm. If you follow these principles you will undoubtedly get 'the firm you want'.

Remember an effective firm can give you the time, financial and mind freedom you want. There are six main things you must focus on.

The first is **you**. Without you understanding yourself, it will be an uphill battle. Make sure you know what you want and then act in a way that will give you the business you want.

Team is the thing you must get right. Without your A-Team, you will have no chance of creating the accounting or bookkeeping firm you want.

The **Rhythm of the business** is simple to do but is something that you must put in place and then follow religiously, whatever you decide your rhythm is. Even if sometimes you think it is overkill, do not stop it.

Business structure is a must to understand and ensure all your team has clarity. Get the systems and procedures all written up and constantly improved on.

The final thing that could make a massive difference in helping you to get **the firm you want** is creating an **offshore team.**

Offshoring can play a significant role in ensuring you get the accounting or bookkeeping firm you want, just as it has for me with Naylor Accountancy Services and other Intelligent Outsourcing partners.

123

I wish you all the best in creating **The Firm You Want,** and if you have already got it, do not sit back on your laurels and ensure you always keep improving.

Appendix

a) Why #hamster?

You may have noticed my headline on LinkedIn is "Let us be your **Hamster** and save you time to grow your business or allow you to breathe" and that I use **#hamster** for sign-off on LinkedIn.

You will no doubt think it is odd. You may think Nikolai Naylor is an accountant with an accountancy firm and an outsourcing offshore business, so why on earth would he use #hamster and have such a weird headline?

Lucky #hamster in 'Hamsterdam' 2023

So let me tell you the story behind #hamster.

I talk to a lot of accountants, and the two things most complain about are:

1. Working too many hours and running around like a 'hamster' in a wheel to talk to clients and get all the work done.
2. Not able to find accountants to take on the compliance work.

Several accountants have said, "I am running around like a **hamster** in a wheel." I started to reply, "Let Intelligent Outsourcing be your **hamster** and do all your compliance work, so you can focus on your clients and delivering added value work."

That led to me creating the LinkedIn headline "Let us be your hamster and save you time to grow your business or allow you to breathe", as this resonated with the pain that we can help alleviate for accountants.

Then the simple **#hamster** sign-off on posts was created. You will also see the rest of Intelligent Outsourcing using #hamster.

I hope you can now see the logic behind the use of #hamster.

The great thing is that everyone can easily remember **#hamster** as it is short and distinctive for an outsourcing offshore business. I have even been called 'the hamster guy' by someone. I'm not sure if this is a good thing or not!

#hamster has been named 'Lucky', chosen from several names suggested by accountancy and bookkeeping firm owners. We did this selection live on LinkedIn using a wheel of names.

*#hamster was named **Lucky** by Lenah Odour*

b) Selling Your Firm?

If you aim to sell your accountancy or bookkeeping firm, it is worth doing all you can to ensure there isn't an issue when you step down. Remember that a buyer will look to clawback lost revenue from you if clients leave the firm within the first two years of the sale.

With Naylor Accountancy Services, we have done one acquisition already and are looking to complete the next one soon. We will then be looking to make an acquisition per year, as with Intelligent Outsourcing supporting Naylor Accountancy Services we know we can deliver an excellent service, take on new clients en masse and integrate them effectively.

If you want to sell your firm, please contact me, Nikolai Naylor, on LinkedIn, as we will be getting our acquisition pipeline ready for the next ten years. Even if you are not thinking about selling now but are within 10 years it is worth reaching out as we are planning ahead.

If you have an offshore team with Intelligent Outsourcing and you want to sell your accounting or bookkeeping firm, it will be favourable to us and we would place you ahead of other acquisitions in the pipeline.

Acknowledgements

It is incredible when you think of who you would like to thank. There are always so many people that help you along your journey, and we are always learning. I would like to thank everyone I know and have met over my many years on this Earth, as every one of you has had an impact in some way.

I have to start by thanking the one person who pushed me to write this book and ensured I stayed on track, so a massive thank you to Ashley Leeds. His positivity, energy, and great creativity are something I have not come across in another person before, and I feel blessed that our paths have crossed.

Simon Chaplin, my amazing coach and mentor, a giant thanks. He challenged me from when I joined his mastermind group. That was pivotal for helping me change my mindset, and it made me realise that running your accountancy firm is not just about knowing what you need to do tax and compliance-wise. He opened my eyes to new ideas and to books through our speakers and from recommendations from other mastermind members. I was inspired to learn more, change things, and continually self-develop. Simon has also helped me get this book into better shape. I would not be where I am now business wise without Simon.

My family has been immense support throughout running my businesses, with my lovely wife Kate putting up with my long hours at the start and having to sort the children out when I am in the Philippines visiting the Intelligent Outsourcing team out there whilst still having her own stellar career. My daughter Grace inspired me to realise that I can write a book as she has already written three books and she's only 17. My son Christian for always smiling and being a fellow fact nerd and someone I can throw a rugby ball around with.

Without Dee Smith and Christine Sy, there would be no Intelligent Outsourcing, so a massive thank you to both of them.

David Parker inspired me to set up my accountancy firm Naylor Accountancy Services, and helped me at the start, so a massive thanks.

Naylor Accountancy Services and Intelligent Outsourcing teams present and past a big thank you for all their dedication and for helping on the journey.

The Leadership Team of Intelligent Outsourcing and Naylor Accountancy Services, without whom I would be unable to 'let go', and neither business would be growing. So, thanks to Dee Smith, Christine Sy, Korina Cue, Jetaime Villamar, Glenny Pili, Pauline Sebastian, Michael Lewis, Franz Venturina, and Andy Jordan.

My Mastermind group, current and past, have always been open and allowed me to continue to learn from them. I really appreciate their support. Thanks to Philip Knight, Jeremy Buitenhuis, Kim Marlor, Chris Bond, Michael Hemme, Nathan Hopkins, Wijay Kanagasundaram, David Gormer, Paul Meades, Jane Capel, Jo Whitehead, Nicola Sorrell, Stuart Ramsay, and of course, Mark Swindale.

Mark Allen for his stories, advice, and for creating TAG, of which we are founding members. I met Mark at my first accountancy conference, and he has been inspirational on his journey, especially in how he overcame his life-threatening predicament. We also both love Tae Kwon Do.

I want to thank Paul Barnes and James Ashford for being the first to invite me to speak publicly about our Intelligent Outsourcing proposition on the GoProposal webinar in August 2019, 'How, When & Why Should My Accountancy Firm Offshore?' The video has had 680 views which, to me, is a lot.

James Ashford for reaching out and suggesting a more professional design for the book's cover, which you have now. The cover was unanimously agreed to be better than the old one on my LinkedIn post.

Last but by no means least I would like to thank all the Filipino people who are so friendly and smiley and always want to please. I especially think of them when things are tough as I am inspired by their positivity. I am so pleased our community outreaches in the region touch the lives of those who have so very little.

Printed in Great Britain
by Amazon

27546040R00086